CHEESE
Hors d'Oeuvres

CHEESE

Hors d'Oeuvres

50 RECIPES FOR CRISPY CANAPÉS,
DELECTABLE DIPS, MARINATED MORSELS,
AND OTHER TASTY TIDBITS

HALLIE HARRON

THE HARVARD COMMON PRESS
BOSTON, MASSACHUSETTS

DEDICATED TO MISS HELOISE WINGS,
WHO CONTINUES TO BE MY CONSTANT SOURCE
OF INSPIRATION AND JOY

The Harvard Common Press
535 Albany Street
Boston, Massachusetts 02118
www.harvardcommonpress.com

Printed in
and on

Library of Congress Cataloging-in-Publication Data
Harron, Hallie
        for crispy canapes, del   le dips,
                and other tasty tidbits / Hallie Harron

Includes index.
ISBN 13: 978-1-55832-371-1 (hbk.)
1. Appetizers.   2. Cookery (Cheese)
TX740.H37   2008
641.8'12   2   2008

Special bulk-order discounts are available on Harvard
Common Press books. Companies and organizations may purchase books
for premiums or resale, or may arrange a custom edition, by contacting
the Marketing Director at the address above.

Book design by Matthew Bouloutian and Vivian Ghazarian
Photography by Jerry Errico
Food styling by Brian Preston-Campbell

10 9 8 7 6 5 4 3 2 1

ACKNOWLEDGMENTS

Thank you again and again, Jay and Fran London, my cheese heads from Arizona—for the testing help, the hints, the tips. Gary and Marilyn Litt, both in the States and in our village, Mollans, *merci bien* for all those wonderful hours spent exploring cheese combos! Hats off also to Jo Weible, another excellent cook; thanks for sharing your wise insights and family recipes. And lastly and so importantly, thanks to Mary Evans, for that constant moral and recipe support. Thank you to all!

CONTENTS

CHEESE BASICS

So many cheeses, so little time! There's more to it

all than *just say cheese*! With so many choices of local and imported
cheeses, how do you know where to begin? That's where I come in. Read
on to get a few basics under your belt, like understanding the terms on
cheese labels, as well as the basic varieties and textures of domestic and
imported cheeses. With that information in hand, along with knowing
which cheeses are best simply eaten and which take well to cooking, and
suggestions for what kinds of cheese to serve when and with what, you'll
be on your way to being a cheese maven before you know it.

Here are a few helpful hints to get you started.

1 **Go native.** That is, head to your local cheese shop and begin there.
Ask for opinions, suggestions, and samples, and try them all; a good
cheese or gourmet shop will happily provide samples to help you
decide. Most cheeses start from cow's, goat's, or sheep's milk. Start
with a sampling of all three types. Begin with mild-tasting cheeses
and move along the spectrum to more fragrant, older, moldier, and
sturdier cheeses. Then start making choices of your own.

2 Go for different colors and shapes. Try fresh, pristine white rounds alongside gray, blue, orange, and yellow logs, squares, and pyramids. And try different textures! Look for soft, creamy, semi-runny cheeses, as well as firmer slicing and harder grating cheeses. Cheese labels often indicate soft, semi-soft, semi-firm, and firm.

3 Go global. Many supermarkets and certainly a good cheese shop will offer you choices from around the globe. Start at home and look for any local cheesemakers—artisanal cheesemaking is growing in the United States. Often you can mail-order wares from cheesemakers in other states. Then branch out to France, Italy, Spain, Germany, Switzerland, England, Mexico, Canada, New Zealand, etc. The list goes on to include all the variations and different regional choices within countries, so be prepared for a delicious and endless frolic.

Cheese mavens, just like wine lovers, often use specialty cheese lingo for different textures. It's handy to become familiar with a few of them, so take several moments to become friends with these few terms.

- **Soft:** These cheeses are usually "right out of the hopper" and have been aged for a very short period of time, if at all. Some locally made cheeses can even be eaten with a spoon, as you would yogurt. Soft cheese also refers to types that are spreadable, such as Camembert or Brie.
- **Semi-soft:** This refers to an aged cheese that is still moist. It can be either spreadable when cut, such as a young Bel Paese, or crumbly, such as many domestic blues. Both are labeled "semi-soft."
- **Semi-firm:** This is a cheese that slices evenly, such as Madrigal Swiss, Jarlsberg, cheddar, or Monterey Jack. These are best cut into wedges, cubes, or paper-thin slices.
- **Firm:** This can also be considered a "slicing" cheese or, if really firm, can be used for grating, such as a Parmesan, aged Asiago, Jack, or manchego.
- **Whey cheese:** Some cheeses are produced by cooking and reducing the whey. Perhaps the most common of these is ricotta ("re-cooked") cheese. Another whey cheese is Norwegian Gjetost, where the liquid is boiled down to produce a caramelized brown product.
- **Pasta filata:** Italian mozzarella, provolone, and caciocavallo are the best examples of the cheesemaking technique called *pasta filata.* The term, which means "spun paste," refers to the process of kneading and stretching the curds into various shapes and sizes of cheese.

10

The rind is a protective coating that keeps the cheese from drying out. Types of cheese rinds are:

- **Natural:** A natural rind that simply forms as the cheese ages can be almost indiscernible until the cheese is really mature. Most blue cheeses, goat cheeses, British farmhouse cheddar, Cheshire, and Gloucester have natural rinds.
- **Bloomy:** A bloomy or "flowery" rind indicates that the cheese has developed mold on the surface. This is visible on soft ripening cheeses, and these cheeses normally have a white coating. Examples are Camembert and Brillat-Savarin.
- **Washed:** A washed rind has literally been washed in some sort of liquid, such as wine, brine, beer, or a strong spirit. The resulting cheese is often sticky on the outside. You'll also find that the rind may be dipped in one of a wide variety of ingredients such as natural ash, herbs, or spices. Tallegio, Munster, Epoisses, and Belgian Chimay are all washed-rind cheeses.

What about Pasteurized versus Raw Cheese?

Contrary to what many people think, raw-milk, or unpasteurized, cheeses are not totally uncooked; they are simply heated to a lower temperature than are pasteurized products. The milk for these cheeses is heated to less than 100°F. They can be young or aged. At the present time, we in the United States are unable to purchase raw-milk cheeses that have been aged for less than 60 days, whereas in Europe, younger raw-milk cheeses are widely available.

When the milk has been heated to over 145°F for a specified amount of time, this qualifies it as a pasteurized product with no possible harmful bacteria. However, cheesemakers generally agree that heating the milk to a higher temperature can compromise the flavor. Small producers, especially in Europe, often use a longer and more flavorful (and lower yield) low-heat approach to production.

Cheese: One Big Extended Family

In the world of cheese, there are several types of classifications. Within each group, there are scores of variations and tastes. It's a good idea to familiarize yourself with a few examples in each of these basic groups.

CREAM? DOUBLE CREAM? TRIPLE CREAM?

Some labels identify cheese as double or triple cream. This refers to the fat content. Double-cream cheeses, which include Petit Suisse, Brie, and Camembert, have a minimum of 60 percent enrichment, while triple-cream cheeses have a deliciously whopping 75 percent cream content. St. André and Brillat-Savarin are two classic triple creams—very rich, voluptuous, and buttery.

HOLEY SWISS
The Swiss family of cheeses share in common a hard rind and medium to large holes running through them. As Swiss cheese undergoes the fermentation process, natural gasses within the cheese expand, causing bubbles that eventually form the characteristic holes. Most of these firm cheeses, including Emmenthaler, Gruyère, and domestic Swiss cheeses, have a sweet and nutty flavor and lend themselves to melting as well as slicing.

THE CHEDDARED LOT
Cheddar refers to a village in Somerset in southwest England; this village has been making cheese since the sixteenth century. The difference in the process is that after the milk is heated, it is cut into cubes to drain the whey, then stacked and "turned" or rotated. This cheese is matured for up to 15 months. Domestic cheddars from California to Vermont offer a variety of flavor options from mild to extremely sharp. Also included in the family are the famous English cheeses such as Gloucester, Cheshire, Caerphilly, and even a few blue cheeses.

ON A BLUE NOTE
Blue cheeses are known for the "veins" that run through the cheese, due to a spore of penicillin that is injected into the cheese. The best-known blues, Italian Gorgonzola, French Roquefort, and English Stilton, are famous for their pungent tang. Note that the texture of blue cheeses can vary from buttery to soft to crumbly, and the colors can vary from light blue to green.

MODERN MIXES THAT MATCH
In the last few years, cheesemakers have expanded their creative efforts to mix and match firm and soft cheeses. Examples of mixed cheeses can be found in each of the above groups. You'll find "Fontiago," a delicious blend of Asiago and fontina, as well as all manner of the classic English Stilton, which is now available flavored with caramelized onions, herbs, cranberries, or mango. Other cheeses infused with nuts, mushrooms, truffles, sage, and more are a tasty addition to the cheese

repertoire. These specialty blends are delicious treats and definitely have earned their place alongside the classic varietals, so expect to see more in the future.

Storing Cheese

The best way I've found to store small amounts of cheese is simply to wrap each one in aluminum foil rather than plastic wrap. Unwanted bacteria and mold form more quickly when cheese is stored in plastic. (Waxed paper is fine if you prefer, but I find that it's a little tedious and tends to unwrap easily.) Europeans commonly store cheese in small, airy wooden cabinets, which are placed in a cool, dark area of the pantry. Some cheeses are simply left on the counter. In the United States we tend to want to prevent any and all bacteria, so the fridge is considered the ideal storage place. Do remember to always bring any cheese to room temperature before serving it. The flavor and texture can completely transform if it sits out for only 30 minutes. Ideally, let soft and assertive cheeses sit out for a few hours before serving.

FREEZING CHEESE

Most cheese experts shudder at the thought. Freezing cheese will certainly change its texture. That said, I have found that some of the higher-fat cheeses such as Camembert and Brie, particularly if they are young and firm, will be only slightly altered and fare quite well when thawed. If you have a large quantity of cheese left over from a party, it's perfectly acceptable to freeze it and use it in cooking at a later time. Casseroles, dips, spreads, or any dish in which the cheese is part of a bigger picture rather than served on its own is a perfect place to use up cheeses that might ultimately spoil without freezing.

Armed for Success in the Kitchen

There exists for cheese lovers a whole toy store of gadgets to collect. Some are more useful than others. Here are just a few favorites that I've found are indispensable, affordable, and efficient.

- **Cheese planes:** I am thankful that someone realized that a carpenter's plane might translate to the perfect tool for shredding and grating cheese. This tool has been adapted for kitchen use and has a sturdy, easy-to-grip handle to keep your fingers intact. Planes are available in many sizes, so choose the one that best fits your hand.

- **Knives:** Small "Parmesan" knives can be useful if you're serving a good-sized part of the wheel as part of a buffet appetizer spread.
- **Spreaders:** Decorative small cheese spreaders for use on cheese trays are a lot more aesthetically pleasing than kitchen knives and are available with every possible shape and size handle. These are perfect for fresh and spreadable cheeses.
- **Plates:** A wooden or ceramic cheese plate is handy to serve cheeses on. A large cutting board will work just as well and can be dressed up with paper "cheese leaves," available in specialty shops.
- **Bells:** An old-fashioned cheese bell is a gorgeous sight on a buffet or coffee table. The bottom plate can usually hold up to three small cheese selections. With ripe and runny cheeses, especially in the summer months, the top dome or bell helps to "corral" the cheese as it starts to run at room temperature.
- **Wires:** If you buy large wheels of cheese and want to slice them perfectly, cheese wires are available, which can be useful and a little less dangerous than a sharp knife, especially on very firm rounds that require a good bit of muscle to get through.
- **Food processor:** Become reacquainted with your food processor when preparing cheese appetizers for a large group. Dips and spreads can be made in record time with the processor, and, of course, there's the shredding disk, which can shred vast quantities of firm cheese in just moments.

Create a Topnotch Cheese Plate

Once you've become familiar with a few different textures, colors, and tastes, it will become easy to create a cheese plate that will please even the most diverse palates. One thing to keep in mind is that less can be more, so it's a good idea to showcase only three to five cheeses each time. For example, for newcomers to goat cheese, start with a fresh, mild round from California or perhaps a local source. This can sit next to a sharper and firmer cheddar, or, if goat cheese is the theme, try a goat Brie or firmer goat Gouda. Then you'll need a soft yet assertive cheese to go with those. Perhaps a ripe cow's milk triple cream or creamy blue. As long as you offer mild, medium, and stronger flavor choices and soft, medium, and firm textures and pay some attention to color and shape, you'll be able to build a dazzling cheese plate. The beauty of this is that the presentation, colors, and combinations of flavors and textures can change every time, and there need be no lemon in the lot!

Once you decide just what's going on the platter, it's time to consider the cracker, crouton, chip, or fruit to serve with the cheeses. With strong, assertive cheeses, the simplest vehicle is usually the best choice, such as thinly sliced baguettes or water crackers. Milder cheeses, like fresh mozzarella and soft goat cheese, can be enhanced by savory biscuits or saltier wafers and crackers. Fall pears love cheese, as do summer berries and grapes in all seasons. These sweeter garnishes complement the salty flavor of many cheeses. Delightful combos include a bite of English Stilton with a pear slice or a ripe berry served with soft goat cheese. Again, there are so many choices. Choose only a few to best highlight the cheeses and garnish the platter.

There are also many condiments that can further enhance your cheese platter. Besides fruit, honey is often served with young, fresh goat cheese or medium-flavored hard cheeses. Mild yet distinctive honey made from flowers such as lavender or orange blossom is a welcome combination. Membrillo or quince paste, a very thick fruit gel, can be a wonderful contrast to stronger, tangy, and salty cheeses, as can its cousin, fig paste. For Italian cheese platters, try serving a bowl of the distinctive mostarda alongside; this is fruit that has been preserved in a sweet syrup containing mustard seed. Last, when in doubt, a few imported olives will always fit the bill and complement most any cheese tray.

Cooking It Up

Cooking with cheese has only a few rules to follow. Once you know the ropes, it's easy to figure out which cheeses work best where.

- **On the grill:** This can be slightly tricky if you're making skewers of meats and vegetables and want to include cheese. Look for "grilling" cheeses like Greek halloumi, which holds its shape and will adhere to the skewer. If you want to include a softer cheese, try grilling the skewers and then adding on the cubes of cheese at the end, just before serving. Small goat cheeses wrapped in grape leaves or aluminum foil can be grilled directly and served on small plates. Melting cheeses like Monterey Jack and mozzarella are fine on the grill as long as they are housed in a vegetable such as a firm bell pepper or tomato, or perched atop a sturdy pizza crust. Be careful to maintain a constant watch on the softer cheeses to avoid having them oozing down the grate and creating a gooey mess.

- **In the oven:** Anyone who loves pizza knows the familiar joy of a mouthful of molten mozzarella just out of the oven. Some cheeses, like mozzarella, provolone, fontina, and Emmenthaler, are born and bred to melt. Remember that once the cheese has melted and is still white or yellow in color, it can be removed from the oven several minutes before serving. Use your broiler to brown the cheese if necessary. In any case, do wait a few moments before passing it around, as hot cheese has been known to sear many a zealous cheese lover's mouth.

- **On the stovetop:** The best way to melt cheese is either in a double boiler or, if you're making fondue, right in the pot. Depending on the type of cheese, especially for fondue, which will be served molten and has to stay that way, it may be necessary to add a small amount of flour or cornstarch to keep the texture from becoming too runny or the cheese from separating.

TIPS ON CHEESY DIPS

Depending on how big the crowd and how diverse the menu, how much dip to make can be perplexing. A general rule of thumb is about ¼ cup per person when there are a few other cheese offerings. Trust me, it's easy to make way too much. That could be the best news, though, as many dips thicken as they stand for a day or two and then make marvelous sandwich fillings. Thinner dips can often be used as salad dressings, marinades, or toppings on grilled poultry, meat, and fish. So if you end up with a bucket of dip left over, you may have caught the brass ring.

Know that most dips in this book can be made a day or so in advance, which is good news for the host and cook. Just remember that dips also taste better at room temperature rather than stone cold, so let them warm up before serving.

Get the right grip on the dip. The right choice for dippers is as important as the dip itself. It's disconcerting to see a beautiful dip on a table littered with the broken and collapsed chips of frustrated dip-eaters. The same principle holds with a carrot stuck into a very thin dip: you will see dip drips all over the surrounding table and floor. Sturdy dips require thick chips, solid bread rounds, and bagel chips, along with celery and veggie sticks. Flowing, thinner dips are best scooped up with thin crisps, crispy flatbreads, and all types of wafer crackers and soft bread rounds.

Cheese and Adult Beverages

Cheese lends itself perfectly to many types of wine, both dry and sweet, as well as beer, hearty ale, fortified cider, and, naturally, Champagne.

It's also a great companion to many cocktails and spirits. Chances are you'll know your crowd and be able to pair cheese treats that combine well with whatever beverages you choose to serve. Try a few of the following classic matches when you're first getting started, then bend those rules like crazy and come up with your own favorites.

Red wine has always been the benchmark for strong cheeses. It's the type of wine generally served during a classic cheese course in a French meal. Fresher, milder cheeses go well with white wine. Especially in the summer months, try a dry Sauvignon Blanc like Sancerre with mild or aged goat cheese crottins. Semi-firm cheeses can also be at home with a slightly sweeter white wine like a Riesling. To really know just which wines best accompany your cheese selections, it would be ideal to taste every wine and every cheese together. In other words, a lifetime hobby! Perhaps a more practical approach is to ask a local wine merchant to help you make selections to complement your cheeses.

Cheese loves beer, and beer drinkers usually love cheese! With so many domestic and global choices available, there are as many options as wine. Generally, a strong brew such as a sharp, bitter India Pale Ale is wonderful with stronger cheeses like aged cheddars. Milder beer, such as lager, is a good match for milder cheeses such as *queso fresco* or any soft and fresh cow's cheese. Pilsner and Brie are welcome together, as are ale and Swiss. Again, let your palate guide you to your favorite combos.

Bubbly adores cheese. Both Champagne and other sparkling beverages, including only slightly sweet hard cider, are good with a variety of cheeses and are especially well suited to little baked tidbits such as gougères (French savory cheese pastry puffs) and cheese palmiers, which are rich little pastries that help tame the bubbles.

With a tray of Mimosas, Margaritas, or Martinis, cheese in almost any guise can be well served and well received. Whether it's an ethnic platter of Mexican Cotijo and chips with beer, a chic imported cheese spread on homemade croutons with sparkling wine, or an old-fashioned cheese ball and saltines with a fruity red wine, the spirit world and the cheese world work happily hand in hand.

What you've just read—how to choose cheese, buy it, store it, and cook with it, and what tools to have on hand—are really just basic smarts. You'll soon have your own expert opinions on how to eat it and what to drink with your favorite *fromage*. In the end you'll say, as I do: *Cheese and Cheers!*

SIMPLE CANAPÉS AND MARINATED CHEESES

Fig and Goat Cheese Crostini

MAKES 16 CROSTINI

CHEESE CHOICES:
A soft, rich Mahon from Minorca, Spain, is a good substitute for the goat cheese.

This is a four-season winner. Whether you use sweet fresh figs in summer or marinated dried figs in the dead of winter, the combination of salty and sweet creates the perfect little bite to serve with chilled Champagne. Make the bread rounds a day ahead by slicing a slightly stale baguette and toasting the rounds in a hot oven for about 10 minutes.

8 fresh or dried Black Mission figs, quartered

½ cup fruity white wine (if using dried figs)

Sixteen ¼-inch-thick slices French baguette, toasted

One 8-ounce fresh goat cheese roll, cut into 8 rounds, rounds halved

1   If using dried figs, soak them in the wine for about 2 hours.

2   Place the bread rounds on a serving platter. Top each one with a half-round of the cheese, followed by 2 fig quarters.

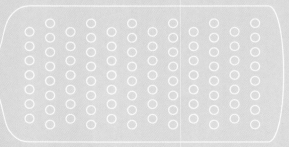

Parmesan and Shrimp Crostini

MAKES 16 CROSTINI

Here's an updated twist on the classic shrimp toast, inspired by an episode of *The Sopranos* that featured a huge gathering of *la famiglia*. Creating true Sicilian flavor is effortless in this appetizer. Make the shrimp mixture up to two days ahead and assemble the crostini when your gang arrives. Top with fresh basil leaves, if you have them on hand.

4 ounces cooked medium-size shrimp

1 tablespoon mayonnaise

1 tablespoon homemade or store-bought basil pesto

1 tablespoon fresh lemon juice

⅓ cup finely shredded Parmesan cheese (about 1 ounce)

Sea salt and freshly ground black pepper to taste

16 thin slices fresh French baguette

1 Preheat the oven to 350°F. Coat a baking sheet with nonstick cooking spray.

2 Place the shrimp, mayonnaise, pesto, lemon juice, and Parmesan in a food processor and pulse until the mixture is chopped but still slightly chunky. Remove to a small mixing bowl, taste, and season with salt and pepper.

3 Place the bread slices on the baking sheet and top each one with a scant tablespoon of the shrimp mixture. Bake for 10 minutes, or until slightly bubbly. Serve warm.

Mascarpone, Hazelnut, and Arugula Canapés

MAKES 24 CANAPÉS

CHEESE CHOICES:
Cream cheese or any triple-cream cheese can be used instead of the mascarpone.

This appetizer is inspired by the offerings of a well-known kiosk in a northern California farmers' market, where arugula, fresh nuts in the shell, boutique cheeses, and organic flatbreads are in abundance. This appetizer just makes itself on the West Coast. The best news, though, is that all of the ingredients are easy to find no matter where you live. Look for cranberry flatbread at Trader Joe's, or use any hearty German-style flatbread.

8 ounces mascarpone cheese (1 cup)

¾ cup skinned, toasted, and chopped hazelnuts

1 small bunch arugula, coarsely chopped

2 tablespoons hazelnut oil

Sea salt and freshly ground black pepper to taste

12 thin slices cranberry flatbread, sliced in half diagonally, or 24 thin slices French baguette, toasted

1 Place the mascarpone in a medium-size bowl and beat with a fork or whisk until creamy. Stir in ½ cup of the nuts. Stir in all but 2 tablespoons of the arugula. Stir in 1 tablespoon of the oil, and season to taste with salt and pepper.

2 Spoon the mixture onto the bread slices and sprinkle the remaining oil, arugula, and hazelnuts over the top.

Wild Mushroom and Blue Cheese Finger Sandwiches

This meaty appetizer is good enough to serve as a whole meal, so feel free to double the recipe and enjoy open-faced sandwiches the next day. If you're a blue cheese fanatic, then increase the amount, keeping the total amount of cheese the same. But beware! Different blue cheeses have different levels of saltiness, so taste and use your own judgment to decide how much to use.

MAKES 12 SANDWICHES

CHEESE CHOICES:
Substitute Havarti for the Jack and a flavorful Maytag blue for the Gorgonzola.

1 ounce dried porcini mushrooms

1½ cups warm water

2 tablespoons extra-virgin olive oil

1 shallot, minced

1 clove garlic, minced

1 teaspoon herbes de Provence

¾ cup stemmed and chopped shiitake mushrooms

1 small bunch fresh chives, minced

Sea salt and freshly ground black pepper to taste

⅓ cup shredded mild Monterey Jack cheese (about 1½ ounces)

⅓ cup crumbled Gorgonzola cheese (about 1½ ounces)

12 thin slices fresh French baguette

1 To rehydrate the porcini mushrooms, soak them in the water for 20 to 30 minutes, or until softened. Drain well.

2 Preheat the broiler.

3 Heat the olive oil over medium heat in a large skillet. Sauté the shallot for 2 minutes, or until lightly colored. Stir in the garlic, herbes de Provence, and shiitake and porcini mushrooms. Cook until the mushrooms are soft, about 5 minutes.

4   Remove from the heat and stir in half of the chives. Season with salt and pepper.

5   Let the mixture cool, then stir in the cheeses. Mound a generous tablespoon of the mixture on each of the bread slices and broil until just bubbly, 1 to 2 minutes. Sprinkle with the remaining chives and place on a serving platter. Serve immediately.

Canapés of Sheep's Milk Cheese and Roasted Peppers

MAKES 16 CANAPÉS

CHEESE CHOICES:
Try a Basque shepherd, Petit Suisse, or Brin d'Amour.

This colorful appetizer can be made well in advance and stored at room temperature. Look for German-style seeded flat bread or any dark whole-grain thinly sliced loaf. The malty bread is an excellent vehicle for the sharp cheese. Use a Basque or Spanish sheep's milk cheese for the best results.

One 4- to 7-ounce jar fire-roasted red and yellow peppers, drained

Eight ¼-inch-thick slices dark German-style bread, sliced in half diagonally

1 cup coarsely grated sheep's milk cheese (about 4½ ounces)

1   Slice the peppers into ⅛-inch-thick strips.

2   Top each bread slice with about 1 tablespoon of cheese and carefully place the pepper strips over the cheese. Place on a platter and serve immediately, or cover and store at room temperature for up to 3 hours.

Fresh Cheese Pâté

SERVES 4

This is a recipe to have fun with. Use your favorite nuts, seeds, and seasonings. Keep the proportions the same and go wild! For instance, try walnuts or cashews instead of almonds. The combination of mild cream cheese and strong blue cheese can also be varied with goat cheese, milder blue cheeses, or whatever you have on hand. No matter the final ingredients, the pâté is best served at room temperature, so if you do make it ahead, remove it from the refrigerator about an hour before serving.

8 ounces cream cheese, at room temperature

2 teaspoons mixed Italian herbs

⅓ cup toasted slivered almonds

2 tablespoons toasted pumpkin seeds

About ½ cup crumbled Gorgonzola cheese (about 2 ounces)

Crackers or thin slices country bread for serving

1   Line a 2-cup loaf pan (2½ x 3 x 5½ inches) with plastic wrap. Oil the plastic wrap.

2   Beat the cream cheese until soft using a large spoon. Stir in the Italian seasoning and spread ¼ cup of the mixture evenly in the loaf pan. Sprinkle with the almonds.

3   Spread another ¼ cup layer of cream cheese over the almonds, and top with the pumpkin seeds. Top the seeds with the blue cheese, and finish the pâté with the remaining cream cheese. Cover with plastic wrap and refrigerate for 1 day or up to 1 week.

4   Turn the loaf out onto a serving plate and remove the plastic wrap. Serve at room temperature with crackers or bread.

Brie with a Pâté of Olives

SERVES 6

CHEESE CHOICES:
Try a French or domestic Camembert in place of the Brie.

This is the ideal appetizer for cooks who like to play. Try a variety of olives, including niçoise, kalamata, green with herbs, or those chile-spiked ones found at the olive bars in so many supermarkets. For fun, buy a variety of olives and make the olive paste a few different ways. Place the olive pastes in different spots on the Brie, as my friend and cheese expert Jay London did, and enjoy them all! Jay also reported a great serving tip: Freeze the finished cheese for half an hour to make slicing a snap. Then let the slices come to room temperature before serving.

½ cup pitted black Mediterranean olives or other olives of your choice

2 teaspoons drained capers

1 clove garlic

1 tablespoon minced fresh flat-leaf parsley

One 7- to 13-ounce wheel ripe but not runny Brie cheese

1 Place the olives, capers, garlic, and parsley in a food processor and pulse until smooth.

2 Slice the Brie in half horizontally to create two rounds. Spread the olive puree on the cut side of the bottom circle and top with the other circle. Wrap well, refrigerate, and let the cheese marinate for 1 day. Slice into small wedges and serve at room temperature.

Marinated Mozzarella Wrapped in Prosciutto

SERVES 4

Ecco! Here's the five-minute appetizer that works any time, any season, and for almost any occasion. Make as many platters as your refrigerator will hold and store them, covered, for up to one day after assembling. Just make sure that you serve these tidbits at room temperature for the best flavor and texture.

CHEESE CHOICES: Smoked mozzarella is a bold and flavorful substitute for the fresh.

8 fresh basil leaves

8 ounces fresh mozzarella cheese, cut into 8 medallions

4 ounces prosciutto, each slice cut in half lengthwise

Extra-virgin olive oil to taste

Freshly ground black pepper to taste

1 Place 1 basil leaf on top of each cheese medallion. Wrap the slices in the prosciutto and place on a serving platter.

2 Drizzle the slices with olive oil and season with pepper.

Marinated Feta and Olives

SERVES 8

Years ago, while living in Marina di Ragusa, Sicily, I discovered olives with fennel seeds and orange zest in the local market. I've made them now for more than 20 years and usually have a stash in the refrigerator. Recently I tried adding feta cheese to the mixture, and *wow*! The marinade worked even more beautifully with both cheese and olives.

1 tablespoon fennel seeds

1 tablespoon cumin seeds

½ teaspoon red pepper flakes, or to taste

2 cloves garlic, minced

Zest of 1 orange

Zest of 1 lemon

2 tablespoons minced fresh basil

8 ounces firm feta cheese, cubed

2 cups pitted kalamata olives

1 Mix together all of the ingredients in a large bowl. Cover and refrigerate for at least 1 day.

2 Serve the mixture at room temperature on small plates from the bowl, or spear the feta cubes with toothpicks and place on a platter surrounded by the olives.

Stilton Marinated in Port

SERVES 6

How simple is this? More is indeed less here, yet take the time to buy the best Stilton and port you can find in your area to get an over-the-moon result. Depending on the ripeness, true English Stilton will vary in its "crumbliness." No matter. Both really crumbly ripe bits and firmer cubes are heavenly when marinated in port wine. You'll see the color change to mauve after just a few hours; however, the peak of the flavor is ideal after one day, so hold off on serving until then.

8 ounces English Stilton (with rind), cubed or crumbled

½ cup ruby port

Water crackers or baguette slices for serving

1   Place the cheese in a medium-size bowl and pour the wine over the top. Cover and let marinate in the refrigerator for 1 day.

2   To serve, place the cheese in a serving bowl and accompany with water crackers or bread slices. Serve at room temperature.

Manchego Marinated in Red Wine and Herbs

SERVES 6

Living in a small village in southern France, we are last on the list to see American art films. So, after finally seeing *Sideways*, the film based in Santa Barbara, California, we "honored" the film by creating a simple appetizer of our local cheese soaked in red wine. Our "Rhône rangers" loved this appetizer, and we've continued to make it ever since. Serve this on a platter with other cheeses, olives or pâté, and crackers.

2 sprigs fresh rosemary

2 sprigs fresh oregano

2 sprigs fresh thyme

1 tablespoon whole black peppercorns

12 ounces manchego cheese, cubed

¾ cup dry red wine

1 Put the herb sprigs and peppercorns in a large bowl. Add the cheese and wine, cover, and refrigerate for 1 day.

2 Pour the mixture through a strainer, then skewer the cheese cubes with toothpicks and place on a platter.

FRIED AND GRILLED CHEESE GOODIES

Cheese Beignets with an Olive and a Twist, recipe on page 36

Cheese Beignets with an Olive and a Twist

These little mouthfuls of crispy pastry have a hidden agenda. You'll find a pungent olive in the center that makes them a must for adventuresome cooks. Serve a tray of perfectly stirred—not shaken—Martinis or, for that matter, flutes of bubbly.

MAKES 24 BEIGNETS

CHEESE CHOICES:
Gruyère or Comté make fine alternatives.

1 cup water

6 tablespoons (¾ stick) butter

¼ teaspoon salt

Freshly ground black pepper to taste

1 cup all-purpose flour

4 large eggs

½ cup grated Jarlsberg or Emmenthaler cheese (about 2 ounces)

½ cup grated Parmesan cheese (about 1⅔ ounces)

1½ cups fresh or dried bread crumbs

24 pitted kalamata olives

1 quart canola oil, for frying

1 In a medium-size saucepan over medium-high heat, bring the water, butter, salt, and pepper to a boil. Remove from the heat and stir in the flour all at once. When well blended, return the pan to the heat. Stir constantly until the dough is very dry and leaves a light film on the pan, about 1 minute. Remove from the heat and let cool for 2 minutes, then beat in the eggs, 1 at a time. Stir in the cheeses.

2 Place the bread crumbs on a plate and drop tablespoonfuls of the mixture on the crumbs, turning to lightly coat all over. Press an olive into the middle of each dough ball and press the dough up and over to completely cover the olive, pinching to seal the top. Recrumb any areas where the crumbs were pushed inside.

3 Heat the oil in a medium-size heavy saucepan to 375°F. Fry the beignets, a few at a time, until browned, 2 to 3 minutes. Remove and drain on paper towels. Serve immediately. Or, let cool and refrigerate; reheat at 350°F for 10 minutes before serving.

Saganaki

SERVES 4

Opa! That's what you'll hear nearly every time you go to a Greek restaurant and someone orders flaming saganaki. You can bring the Greek isles into your own backyard or dining room with this simple recipe. You'll love the dramatic result.

2 large eggs

3 tablespoons all-purpose flour

8 ounces Greek kasseri cheese, cut into 2-inch squares

2 tablespoons extra-virgin olive oil

3 tablespoons Cognac or brandy

1 lemon, quartered

1 Place the eggs in a shallow bowl and beat until blended. Place the flour on a large plate. Dip the cheese squares into the eggs, then coat lightly with the flour.

2 Heat the oil in a large nonstick skillet over medium-high heat. Sauté the cheese until golden, 1 to 2 minutes on each side.

3 Remove from the heat and add the Cognac. Carefully ignite the Cognac with a long match and bring the flaming skillet to the table. When the flames subside, immediately squeeze the lemon quarters over the dish and serve.

Sausage and Cheese Mini Brochettes

MAKES 8 SKEWERS

I first spied this little Greek meze in a "summer entertaining"–themed French supermarket case. These mini brochettes were ready to grill. The salty halloumi cheese hails from Cyprus. It's quite extraordinary in that this cheese can be grilled, baked, or fried without really melting, making for a handy appetizer.

4 precooked turkey sausage links

1 medium-size red bell pepper, cut into 1-inch cubes

4 ounces halloumi cheese, cut into ½-inch cubes

Eight 6-inch wooden skewers, soaked in water for 30 minutes

1   Prepare a medium fire in a grill.

2   Cut each sausage into 4 pieces. Make the skewers by placing a sausage round on a skewer, followed by a pepper square and a cheese cube, and finish with another sausage round.

3   Grill until browned, 2 to 3 minutes per side. Serve hot.

Warm Camembert and Apple Appetizers

SERVES 6 TO 8

This appetizer is the darling of our fall cooking school program in Mollans-sur-Ouvèze, France. We are fortunate to get Chanticleer apples, and heavenly Camembert is only 1 euro! It's a little more expensive on this side of the pond, but worth every dime. Feel free to substitute a ripe Brie if you prefer. Make and slice everything ahead, and simply rewarm the apples gently before serving. Provide toothpicks for skewering.

One 7- to 13-ounce round ripe Camembert cheese, at room temperature

2 tablespoons unsalted butter

2 Golden Delicious or Gala apples, cored and coarsely chopped (no need to peel)

1 teaspoon confectioners' sugar

1 Cut the Camembert into ¾-inch chunks or wedges.

2 Melt the butter over medium heat in a medium-size skillet. Add the apples and cook for about 5 minutes, or until the apples just begin to soften. Sprinkle with the sugar, cook for 1 minute longer, and remove from the heat.

3 Spear an apple piece and a piece of cheese on a toothpick and arrange on a serving platter. Or, assemble a platter with the cheese pieces and a small bowl with the apples, and toothpicks on the side. Serve warm or at room temperature.

Italian Pasta Croccante

SERVES 8

Here is an Italian takeoff on nachos, made with fresh pasta that's topped with Parmesan and pesto. Feel free to use any color of pasta. The spinach variety is beautiful when brushed with the pesto; however, regular fresh yellow pasta works just as well. Air bubbles form inside the dough as it fries, making for delightful crunchy pockets to catch the pesto, cheese, and nuts. If you purchase larger pasta sheets, simply cut them to the appropriate size.

1 quart sunflower or canola oil, for deep-frying

8 sheets fresh spinach pasta, cut into 5 x 8-inch rectangles

1 cup homemade or store-bought basil pesto

About ¾ cup shredded Parmesan or Grana Padano cheese (about 2½ ounces)

¼ cup pine nuts, toasted

1   Heat the oil to 375°F in a medium-size saucepan over medium-high heat.

2   While the oil heats, cut the pasta sheets in half on the diagonal to make 16 triangles.

3   When the oil is hot, drop in the pasta chips two at a time. The pasta will sink and then almost immediately rise to the surface. Using metal tongs, press down on the dough to keep it submerged in the oil. Air bubbles will form and the dough will brown in about 3 minutes. Remove and drain well on paper towels. Repeat with the rest of the pasta.

4   Spread each triangle with a scant tablespoon of pesto. Add a sprinkling of cheese and a few nuts. Serve immediately.

Cayenne-Spiked Chèvre with Cherry Tomatoes

SERVES 8

Here's a colorful gem to make in the height of summer tomato season. Jay London, who lives for delicious cheese and homemade breads, tried this with his homemade focaccia and several colors of tomatoes. The dish ended up being an entire meal for him and his wife, Fran! Even with a store-bought loaf, this is a winner.

1 loaf focaccia (about 2 pounds), cut into thick wedges

8 ounces fresh goat cheese, at room temperature

1 pint multicolor or red cherry tomatoes, halved

1 teaspoon smoked paprika

Cayenne pepper to taste

Fleur de sel or other sea salt to taste

2 tablespoons garlic-flavored extra-virgin olive oil

1 Preheat the broiler.

2 Place the bread wedges on a baking sheet and spread the cheese over the top of the slices. Top with the tomatoes and sprinkle with the paprika and cayenne.

3 Broil for 3 to 4 minutes, or until the cheese is just molten. Remove from the oven, sprinkle with salt, and top each wedge with a drizzle of oil. Serve immediately.

Grilled Shiitakes with Taleggio

SERVES 4

CHEESE CHOICES:
Use a soft Italian fontina instead of the Taleggio.

I first sampled this with a friend in a trattoria in Civitavecchia, near Rome. It was fresh porcini season, and when we'd finished, we ordered two more plates! The warm cheese on the mushrooms was just divine! Shiitake mushrooms are a little more austere than porcinis, but they taste great with a nice ripe Taleggio cheese. Feel free to try this also with portobello or cremini mushrooms.

2 tablespoons extra-virgin olive oil

1 clove garlic, minced

1 tablespoon minced fresh flat-leaf parsley

Sea salt and freshly ground black pepper to taste

8 shiitake mushrooms (1½ to 2 inches in diameter), stemmed

4 ounces soft Italian Taleggio cheese, cut into 8 pieces

1   Prepare a medium fire in a grill, or preheat the broiler.

2   In a small mixing bowl, mix together the oil, garlic, and parsley. Season with salt and pepper, and rub the mushrooms on both sides with the oil mixture.

3   Place a piece of cheese on each mushroom and place the mushrooms on an oiled baking sheet. Grill or broil the mushrooms until the cheese melts, 2 to 3 minutes. If you have a grill rack, place the mushrooms directly on the grill; otherwise, place the baking sheet on the grill. Serve piping hot.

California Crostini

MAKES 8 CROSTINI

CHEESE CHOICES:
Try to find a local blue cheese. Equally delicious with the polenta is a ripe Taleggio or a French Camembert.

Leave it to California to offer Mediterranean delights with a minimum of simple, yet fetching, flavors. First tasted in my favorite little trattoria, Da Vito in San Diego, California, this hors d'oeuvre will showcase your favorite blue cheese from California, Italy, or France. It's really easy to find precooked polenta these days, which makes for a treat that's ready in less than 10 minutes. For a fancier touch, cut the polenta into shapes with a cookie cutter.

2 tablespoons extra-virgin olive oil

One 1-pound roll precooked polenta, cut into eight ⅓-inch-thick slices

4 ounces creamy blue cheese, cubed or crumbled

⅓ cup finely chopped walnuts

1   Heat the olive oil in a large nonstick skillet. Sauté the polenta slices for 3 minutes on each side, or until lightly browned.

2   Top each round with a tablespoon of the cheese, and sprinkle the cheese with the nuts.

3   Transfer to a serving platter and serve immediately.

So-Cal Quesadillas with Queso Fresco and Avocado

SERVES 4 TO 8

CHEESE CHOICES:
If *queso fresco* is unavailable where you are, substitute shredded whole-milk mozzarella cheese, or even crumbled feta.

Avocados are what inspired the "So-Cal," or Southern California, title of this recipe. In the hills above Santa Barbara and all around San Diego, avocado orchards abound, and the fruit is considered a dietary staple!

Canola oil

Four 10-inch flour tortillas

8 ounces *queso fresco*, crumbled (about 1 cup)

1 large ripe Hass avocado, pitted, peeled, and cubed

1½ cups fresh tomato salsa

1   Coat a stovetop griddle with oil and heat over medium heat until almost smoking. Add 1 tortilla and sprinkle ¼ of the cheese and a few avocado cubes over half of the tortilla. Fold the tortilla in half and press the edges lightly together. Brown over medium heat for 1 to 2 minutes, then turn the quesadilla and brown the other side until golden, about 1 minute.

2   Remove from the heat and place on a paper towel to cool slightly. Repeat with the remaining tortillas, adding more oil to the griddle as needed. Slice each quesadilla into 4 wedges and serve warm on a platter with a bowl of salsa.

The Best Grilled Cheese: A Tartine

SERVES 4

It's easy to have homemade cheese blends on hand for quick appetizers. Here's one combo from the food court under the Louvre museum, where one little café sells several of its own cheese blends. Using the blends, the kiosk also cranks out more than 1,000 of these tartines an hour during the lunch crunch. No wonder! After a morning of museum exhibits and shopping, a tartine and a glass of chilled wine can be so restorative.

1 small baguette, cut diagonally into eight ⅓-inch-thick slices

One 5.2-ounce package Boursin cheese

4 ounces prosciutto

⅓ cup shredded young Asiago cheese (about 1½ ounces)

⅓ cup shredded young provolone cheese (about 1½ ounces)

⅓ cup shredded fontina cheese (about 1½ ounces)

¼ cup minced fresh chives

1   Prepare a medium fire in a grill, or preheat the broiler.

2   Spread each bread slice with a scant tablespoon of the Boursin. Top with the prosciutto.

3   Mix the Asiago, provolone, and fontina cheeses together in a small bowl. Divide the three-cheese mixture over the prosciutto, using about 2 tablespoons for each bread slice.

4   Grill until the cheese is melted and molten. Cool slightly, then sprinkle with chives and serve immediately.

Fried Cheese Curds

SERVES 6

If you're from the Midwest, there is hardly need of explanation of fried fresh cheese curds. They are the must-eat snack at every state fair in Minnesota and, of course, Wisconsin. For those of you unfamiliar with this treat, curds are knobby-shaped, randomly sized bits of natural fresh cheddar cheese, sold within a few days of production. Fresh curds can be ordered from specialty cheese shops almost anywhere. You can substitute milk or water for the beer, if you like.

1 quart sunflower or canola oil, for deep-frying

1 pound fresh cheese curds

1 cup all-purpose flour

1 teaspoon baking powder

½ teaspoon salt

Pinch of cayenne pepper

2 large eggs, beaten

½ cup lager-type beer, at room temperature

1   In a medium-size saucepan, heat the oil to 375°F.

2   Separate the curds, if necessary. Mix together the flour, baking powder, salt, and cayenne in a large bowl. Stir together the eggs and beer and gradually add the liquid to the dry ingredients to form a smooth batter, adding a little more beer if the batter is thicker than pancake batter.

3   Dip the curds into the batter, letting the excess batter drip back into the bowl. Fry the curds in small batches, 2 or 3 at a time, for about 1½ minutes, or until golden brown.

4   Drain on paper towels and serve immediately.

BAKED CHEESE BITES

Spinach and Ricotta Tapa

SERVES 6

CHEESE CHOICES:
Try California fromage blanc for the ricotta and Asiago for the feta.

Kudos to my friend Jo Weibel, who adores cheese and has enough family recipes on the subject to write her own book. She shared this Mediterranean appetizer—sort of like a frittata or Spanish tortilla—with me, and I loved it both warm and cold. It is particularly nice with an afternoon glass of dry sherry.

One 10-ounce package chopped frozen spinach, thawed

1 tablespoon extra-virgin olive oil

1 shallot, minced

1 clove garlic, minced

One 15-ounce container whole-milk ricotta cheese

½ cup crumbled feta cheese (about 2 ounces)

3 large eggs, beaten

2 tablespoons minced fresh basil

Sea salt and freshly ground black pepper to taste

1 medium-size ripe tomato, cored and chopped

1   Preheat the oven to 350°F.

2   Squeeze the spinach until all the liquid has been removed. Heat the olive oil in a large skillet over medium-high heat. Add the shallot and sauté for 3 minutes. Add the garlic and spinach, cover, and steam until warmed through, about 2 minutes. Remove from the heat and stir in the cheeses, eggs, and basil. Lightly season with salt and pepper.

3   Spread the mixture in a 9-inch oiled springform pan or other round baking dish. Bake for 15 minutes. Remove from the oven and spoon the chopped tomato over the top. Cut into small wedges and serve on small plates.

Baked Ricotta with Tapenade

SERVES 6

CHEESE CHOICES:
For the sheep's cheese, try manchego from Spain or Vermont, Petit Basque, or aged pecorino.

Here is a French provençal and niçoise specialty, often found in the older food stalls near the famous flower market in Nice. You can buy the whole "terrine" and sit with a baguette on the Promenade des Anglais, or, if you're lucky enough to stay in a spot with a kitchen, just simply purchase all the fixings and make it yourself. The good news is, it's also easy to re-create anywhere here in the States, as tapenade and ricotta are supermarket staples. Serve with sesame crackers or toasted baguette slices.

One 15-ounce container whole-milk ricotta cheese

¼ cup grated or crumbled sheep's milk cheese (about 1 ounce)

2 large eggs, beaten

3 tablespoons prepared tapenade

1 tablespoon minced fresh chives

Freshly ground black pepper to taste

1   Preheat the oven to 375°F. Oil or spray a 2-cup baking dish.

2   Place the ricotta and sheep's milk cheeses in a large bowl. Stir in the eggs, tapenade, and half of the chives. Season generously with pepper. Turn the mixture into the baking dish, smoothing the top.

3   Bake for 20 to 25 minutes, or until browned and slightly puffed yet still a bit jiggly in the center. The dish will deflate as it cools. Scatter the remaining chives on top and serve at room temperature directly from the baking dish. Or, if you like, unmold the ricotta onto a serving dish and scatter the chives on top.

Caramel- ized Onion, Cambozola, and Pear Galette

SERVES 8

CHEESE CHOICES:
A good substitute for the Cambozola is a farmstead blue cheese from Point Reyes, California.

As one tester commented, this is "positively dreamy." The combination of textures and sweet, salty, pungent, and rich flavors makes this new-age pizza a real delight.

½ cup (1 stick) unsalted butter, melted

3 large onions, thinly sliced

Sea salt and freshly ground black pepper to taste

1 tablespoon minced fresh thyme

2 teaspoons sugar

1 tablespoon balsamic vinegar

Two 3-ounce packages cream cheese, at room temperature

10 sheets phyllo dough, thawed if frozen

1 ripe pear, cored and thinly sliced

4 ounces Cambozola or Gorgonzola cheese, rind removed and cubed

½ cup chopped walnuts

1   Preheat the oven to 375°F.

2   Heat 3 tablespoons of the butter in a large skillet over medium heat. Add the onions, season with salt and pepper, and stir in the thyme, sugar, and vinegar. Reduce the heat to medium-low and simmer for about 30 minutes, or until the onions are very tender. Remove from the heat and stir in the cream cheese.

3   Layer the phyllo sheets in a 12-inch tart pan or pizza pan, brushing each sheet lightly with some of the remaining butter. Place the onion-cheese filling on top of the pastry and arrange the pear slices over the top in a circular pattern, leaving a 2½- to 3-inch edge. Top the pears with the cheese cubes and walnuts. Take the edges of the pastry and fold them in toward the center. There will be a "hole" in the center of the pizza. Brush some melted butter over the top. Bake until golden, 30 to 35 minutes. Cool slightly, and cut into small wedges to serve.

Brie Bites

MAKES ABOUT
4½ DOZEN BITES

Welcome to the ultimate easy slice, bake, and serve dough. The recipe is adapted from *sablés*, sweet French biscuits. Try these savory "sandies" with pears and figs in the fall or apricots and peaches in the late spring and summer. *Impeccable!*

2 cups all-purpose flour

1 teaspoon salt

½ teaspoon baking powder

⅛ teaspoon cayenne pepper

¾ cup (1½ sticks) cold unsalted butter, cut into small chunks

4 ounces Brie cheese, rind removed and cubed

1 cup finely chopped walnuts

1 large egg, beaten

1   Place the flour, salt, baking powder, and cayenne in the bowl of a food processor and pulse until blended. Add the butter and pulse to blend into small pieces. Add the cheese and nuts and pulse again, until the cheese is in very small pieces. Add the egg, and pulse until the mixture just starts to come together.

2   Remove the dough to a lightly floured surface. Press the dough together into a ball, then divide into 2 equal-size balls. Pat and roll each ball into a log 7 inches long and 1½ inches in diameter.

3   Wrap each log in plastic wrap and refrigerate for 1 hour or overnight.

4   Preheat the oven to 400°F. Line 2 baking sheets with parchment paper. Slice the logs ¼ inch thick using a serrated knife and place the slices 1 inch apart on the baking sheets. Bake for 10 to 12 minutes, or until the color of sand and the bottoms are very lightly browned. Place on a rack to cool. Serve at room temperature.

Greek Galette with Feta and Mozzarella

SERVES 4 TO 6

CHEESE CHOICES:
If you can find it, try the creamiest and the king of mozzarella, burrata, in place of the regular mozzarella.

Santorini, here we come! A few years ago, during a month of vacation in the Greek isles, I settled in at the local wine bar and had this appetizer almost every day. Sometimes it came with a small bowl of olives. Other times, a saucer of feta or other local cheese in olive oil arrived. I always ordered a glass of the local "red" and thoroughly enjoyed each day of R and R. On your end, enjoy these tastes anywhere you are.

10 sheets phyllo dough, thawed if frozen

¼ cup (½ stick) unsalted butter, melted

About 1 cup coarsely shredded fresh mozzarella cheese (4 ounces)

About ¾ cup crumbled feta cheese (3 ounces)

¼ cup grated Parmesan cheese (about ¾ ounce)

1 tablespoon freshly minced marjoram, or 1½ teaspoons dried marjoram

1 cup chopped green onions (scallions)

1 cup drained, chopped marinated artichoke hearts

1   Preheat the oven to 375°F.

2   Line a 9-inch springform pan with the phyllo, lightly brushing each sheet with butter after you lay it in the pan. Also brush the edges of the pastry, which will overhang the sides of the pan.

3   Spread the mozzarella, feta, and Parmesan cheeses, the marjoram, green onions, and artichokes over the top of the pastry. Fold the overhanging edges of the phyllo in over the topping, and brush the top of the pastry with butter.

4   Bake for 35 to 40 minutes. Cool slightly, remove the sides of the pan, cut the galette into wedges, and serve.

Baked Crab and Cheddar Croutons

SERVES 8

CHEESE CHOICES:
Of course, you may use Boursin in place of the cream cheese.

This is a West Coast favorite during Dungeness crab season. You can save a lot of time and trouble by buying freshly picked crabmeat. Its gloriously sweet taste is a nice match for the slightly pungent cheddar. You could also try blue crab or, in a pinch, canned crabmeat. Note that the crab mixture can be made up to two days ahead and then the croutons topped and baked at the last minute.

¼ pound fresh Dungeness crabmeat (about ¾ cup)

One 5.2 ounce package garlic-herb cream cheese (about ½ cup), at room temperature

1 teaspoon Dijon mustard

2 tablespoons dry sherry

½ cup grated white cheddar cheese (about 2 ounces)

Grated zest of 1 lemon

Tabasco sauce to taste

16 thin slices fresh French baguette

Dill sprigs for garnish

1   Preheat the oven to 350°F.

2   In a large bowl, blend together the crab, cream cheese, mustard, sherry, cheese, lemon zest, and Tabasco sauce.

3   Mound the mixture onto the baguette slices and bake for 10 minutes, or until warmed through and slightly bubbly. Top each crouton with a small dill sprig and serve immediately.

White Cheddar Gougères

MAKES ABOUT
3½ DOZEN GOUGÈRES

CHEESE CHOICES:
For an Italian twist, grate aged provolone instead of cheddar.

If you're lucky enough to find Grafton Village Classic Reserve Extra Aged Vermont Cheddar, then you'll understand what some of the best domestic cheddar cheese is. That said, any good-quality cheddar will work just as well in this appetizer. Whichever cheese you use, make these in quantity ahead of time, and then reheat them any time you need a special cocktail treat.

1 cup all-purpose flour

½ teaspoon dry mustard

1 cup water

6 tablespoons (¾ stick) cold butter

1 teaspoon salt

4 large eggs

1 cup grated sharp white cheddar cheese (about 4 ounces)

1   Preheat the oven to 400°F. Lightly oil 2 baking sheets.

2   In a large bowl, mix together the flour and dry mustard.

3   In a medium-size saucepan, bring the water, butter, and salt to a boil. Remove the pan from the heat and stir in the flour mixture all at once. When well blended, return the pan to the heat. Stir constantly until the dough is very dry and leaves a light film on the pan, about 1 minute. Remove from the heat and let cool for 5 minutes.

4   Beat in the eggs, 1 at a time, blending well after each addition. Stir in the cheese and blend. Drop the dough by rounded teaspoonfuls onto the baking sheets.

5   Bake the first sheet for 25 minutes in the center of the middle rack, or until browned. Remove from the oven and prick each puff with the tip of a knife. Bake for 3 minutes longer, then remove the puffs to a rack to cool. Repeat with the remaining sheet. Serve warm or at room temperature.

Really Goud-a Straws

MAKES ABOUT 24 STRAWS

You might want to double this recipe, as these mini-straws are irresistible. It's the Dutch Gouda that makes the difference and gives these that "something more" quality. The unbaked dough keeps for two months in the freezer, so this is ideal when a last-minute crowd knocks at the door.

4 tablespoons (½ stick) unsalted butter, softened

8 ounces Dutch Gouda cheese, grated (about 2 cups)

¾ cup sifted all-purpose flour

1½ teaspoons baking powder

½ teaspoon salt

½ teaspoon freshly ground black pepper

¼ teaspoon paprika

1   Preheat the oven to 350°F.

2   Beat the butter in a large bowl with a wooden spoon until creamy. Beat in the cheese, flour, baking powder, salt, pepper, and paprika, beating by hand until a soft dough forms.

3   Break off tablespoons of dough and roll each piece into 2½-inch cigar-shaped strips. Place on an ungreased baking sheet. Bake for 35 minutes, or until barely golden brown. Serve at room temperature.

Parmesan Biscotti

Slather on creamy, soft goat cheese for the perfect foil. These are also delicious on their own with a summery aperitif.

MAKES ABOUT 3 DOZEN BISCOTTI

CHEESE CHOICES: Any aged grating cheese, such as Greek mitzithra or Asiago, will work well here.

2½ cups all-purpose flour

½ tablespoon salt

2 teaspoons baking powder

½ cup grated Parmesan cheese (about 1⅔ ounces)

½ cup slivered almonds, toasted

1 tablespoon herbes de Provence

3 tablespoons unsalted butter, softened

4 large eggs

½ cup cold water

1   Preheat the oven to 350°F. Line a baking sheet with parchment paper and lightly coat the parchment with olive oil.

2   In a large bowl, mix together the flour, salt, baking powder, Parmesan, almonds, herbes de Provence, and butter. In a separate bowl, beat together 3 of the eggs with the water. Gradually beat the egg mixture into the flour mixture. Turn the moist dough out onto a floured surface and knead until smooth, about 2 minutes. Form 2 logs about 10 inches long and place on the prepared baking sheet. Beat the remaining egg and brush it over the surface of the logs.

3   Bake for 25 minutes, or until lightly golden. Let cool slightly. Reduce the oven temperature to 325°F. Cut the logs diagonally into ¼-inch-thick slices and lay the slices cut side down on the same baking sheet. Bake for an additional 10 to 15 minutes, or until crisped. Store in a covered container for up to 3 weeks.

Cheddar-Pecorino Crisps with Rosemary

MAKES 24 CRISPS

CHEESE CHOICES:
An excellent cloth-aged Vermont cheddar from Shelburne Farms or an English cheddar can be substituted.

These savory "refrigerator cookies" are great to have in the freezer, either already baked or in a ready-to-slice log. The nutty New Zealand cheddar is a great addition; however, if it is impossible to find in your specialty cheese shop, use any good-quality white cheddar cheese. Try serving a platter of these crisps with an equally crisp Sauvignon Blanc from New Zealand.

1½ cups all-purpose flour

½ cup grated white New Zealand cheddar cheese (about 2 ounces)

¼ cup grated pecorino cheese (about 1 ounce)

Leaves of 1 large sprig fresh rosemary or 2 teaspoons dried rosemary

Leaves of 1 large sprig fresh thyme or 1 teaspoon dried thyme

½ cup (1 stick) cold salted butter, cubed

½ cup sour cream

1 egg yolk

1 Place the flour, cheeses, rosemary, and thyme in the bowl of a food processor and pulse until blended. Add the butter and pulse until the mixture resembles coarse cornmeal.

2 In a small bowl, beat together the sour cream and egg yolk. Add the sour cream mixture to the flour mixture and pulse until it just begins to form into a very sticky dough. Remove the dough, moisten your hands with water, and form a 10-inch-long log. Wrap the dough in plastic wrap and refrigerate or freeze until just firm.

3 Preheat the oven to 375°F. Spray 2 baking sheets with nonstick cooking spray.

4   If the roll has frozen solid, let it thaw for several minutes. Slice the roll into ¼-inch-thick slices and place on the baking sheets. Bake for about 15 minutes. Flip the crisps over and bake for an additional 5 minutes, or until golden brown. Cool the crisps slightly before serving.

Frico

MAKES 24 CHIPS

Who discovered that melted Parmesan makes the most addictive chip in the world? These are sexy and dangerous! They are even more so if you splurge and use the very best Parmigiano-Reggiano or Grana Padano. To ensure the best texture, flatten the little fricos into 2-inch rounds before you bake them. If you have the same idea I did, go ahead and use any leftovers as a garnish for your Caesar salad.

2 cups coarsely grated Parmesan cheese (about 6½ ounces)

2½ tablespoons all-purpose flour

Freshly ground black pepper to taste

1   Preheat the oven to 375°F. Oil 2 nonstick baking sheets.

2   In a large bowl, thoroughly mix the cheese and flour. Season generously with pepper. Place generous tablespoonfuls of the mixture ½ inch apart on the baking sheets, and bake for about 10 minutes, or until fragrant and golden brown.

3   Place the chips on a rack and let cool to room temperature. Serve immediately, store in an airtight container at room temperature for up to 2 days, or freeze for up to 2 weeks.

Mini Stilton Palmiers

MAKES 36 PALMIERS

CHEESE CHOICES:
Try a rich Gorgonzola or the elegant blue from Great Hill Dairy in Massachusetts in place of the Stilton.

It's easy to enjoy these mini pastries with maxi flavor. Stilton is a good cheese choice here, especially if your guests enjoy strong, rich flavors. You may also use Gorgonzola. If you'd like a somewhat milder flavor, try wrapping the pastry around a nutty Gruyère or mild Monterey Jack.

1 sheet frozen puff pastry dough, thawed

1 large egg, beaten

½ cup crumbled English Stilton cheese (about 2 ounces)

1   Unroll the pastry sheet and cut it in half lengthwise (no need to roll it out). Working with one piece at a time, brush the surface edges with the egg, forming a 1-inch border. Scatter half the cheese over the top of the pastry, avoiding the egg-brushed border.

2   Fold in the long sides to meet in the middle of the sheet. With the long side still toward you, fold the top and bottom of the pastry sheet to meet again in the center. Fold the top half over the bottom. Turn the roll over and pinch the ends together to seal. Repeat with the remaining pastry sheet and cheese. Wrap the dough in plastic wrap and freeze for 30 minutes or up to 1 month.

3   Preheat the oven to 400°F. Oil or spray 2 baking sheets.

4   If the roll has frozen solid, let it thaw for 15 minutes before slicing. Cut each roll into ¼-inch-thick slices and place cut side down ½ inch apart on the baking sheets. Bake for 15 minutes, or until golden. Let cool on a rack and serve at room temperature.

Mini Swiss Pinwheels

MAKES ABOUT 36 PINWHEELS

CHEESE CHOICES:
Any good-quality Swiss cheese, including Emmenthaler, can be used here.

This elegant pastry takes only moments to produce and can be frozen for up to three months before baking. Feel free to double or triple the recipe so that you can have a big batch of pinwheels available at a moment's notice. The aged Gruyère is a treat in itself and elevates these little appetizers to "queen-worthy."

⅔ cup grated aged Gruyère cheese (about 3½ ounces)

1 tablespoon mixed Italian herbs

1 sheet frozen puff pastry dough, thawed

1 large egg, beaten

½ cup roasted red peppers, cut into thin strips

1 Mix together the cheese and Italian herbs in a small bowl.

2 Unfold the pastry sheet on a lightly floured surface and cut in half crosswise (no need to roll it out). Brush the surface with the egg. Arrange the pepper strips on top of the two pastry pieces and scatter half of the cheese on each piece. Starting with the long edge nearest to you, roll each pastry sheet into a log. Wrap each in plastic wrap. Freeze for 1 hour or up to 3 months.

3 Preheat the oven to 400°F. Oil or spray 2 baking sheets.

4 Remove the pastry from the freezer and, when easy to cut, slice the logs into ¼-inch-thick slices. Place the pinwheels, cut side down, ¼ inch apart on the prepared sheets and bake for 12 to 15 minutes, or until golden. Remove to a rack, let cool slightly, and serve.

Spicy Cheese Totes

MAKES 12 TOTES

CHEESE CHOICES:
You may use regular Jack or Havarti in place of the pepper Jack when a less-spicy snack is in order.

Need just the peppy bite to go with a pitcher of margaritas? This rich and buttery pastry packs a walloping punch. For extra spice, serve a bowl of hot salsa and a shaker of Tabasco sauce with the totes.

6 sheets phyllo dough, thawed if frozen

½ cup (1 stick) unsalted butter, melted

8 ounces hot pepper Jack cheese, cut into twelve ½-inch-thick slices

12 large green olives stuffed with pimientos or chiles, halved

1   Preheat the oven to 400°F.

2   Brush the first sheet of phyllo with butter. (Keep the other sheets covered so they won't dry out.) Cut the buttered sheet in half lengthwise, then cut each half with scissors crosswise into quarters, to get 8 pieces from the sheet. Stack 4 pieces on top of each other, fanning them out by offsetting the squares. Repeat this with the other 4 pieces. Place a rectangle of cheese in the center of each stack, and top the cheese with 2 olive halves. Bring the edges of the pastry together over the filling and seal them by pinching and pleating the edges together to form a little "tote."

3   Place the pastries on an ungreased baking sheet. Repeat the process with the remaining sheets of phyllo dough. Bake the totes for 12 to 15 minutes, or until browned. Let cool slightly before serving.

CHEESE TO DIP INTO

Hot and Spicy Artichoke Dip

SERVES 6

Here's what to serve with beer and tortilla chips. The combination of creamy cheese and distinctive artichoke flavor goes great with a glass of good lager. This classic dip has been available in sports bars and casual cafés for years. Who knew it was so simple to make at home? This version is as good cold as it is hot, and it keeps in the refrigerator for up to a week.

One 13.75-ounce can water-packed artichoke hearts

One 10-ounce can diced tomatoes with green chiles

8 ounces cream cheese

⅓ cup mayonnaise

½ cup grated Parmesan cheese (about 1⅔ ounces)

Salt and freshly ground black pepper to taste

Hot sauce of your choice, to taste

1   Preheat the oven to 350°F.

2   Place all of the ingredients in a blender and pulse until smooth.

3   Place the mixture in an 8-inch square or other 2-quart baking dish and bake until bubbly, about 30 minutes.

4   Stir the dip and serve piping hot.

Minty Feta Dip with Roasted Garlic

This dip thickens as it sits, so if you make it a few days ahead, you may have to thin it with a little milk or cream. Serve this with pita bread or pita chips. If you prefer to serve it thick, use sturdy croutons and carrot and celery sticks as dippers. Any thick leftovers are stellar sandwich-spread material.

SERVES 8

CHEESE CHOICES:
Any strong and crumbly goat's milk cheese, such as Greek kefalotiri or kasseri, can be used instead of the feta.

2 heads garlic

8 ounces feta cheese with black peppercorns, crumbled (about 2 cups)

½ cup plain Greek-style yogurt

3 tablespoons extra-virgin olive oil, plus extra for garnish

2 tablespoons chopped fresh mint

Salt and freshly ground black pepper to taste

1 Preheat the oven to 350°F.

2 Wrap the garlic heads in aluminum foil and place on a baking sheet. Bake for 45 minutes, or until the heads are very soft when squeezed. Let cool completely. Squeeze the individual cloves into a medium-size bowl.

3 Add the cheese, yogurt, oil, and mint to the bowl and beat until well blended. Season with salt and pepper, sprinkle with the oil, and serve.

Six-Layer South-western Dip

SERVES 8 TO 10

CHEESE CHOICES:
If Mexican cheeses such as soft panela or asadero are available in your area, by all means use them in place of the Jack.

This can be a seven-alarm fire if you like. Or you can tone it down with mild salsa and regular Jack cheese without jalapeños. Whichever version you choose, the result is dramatic when served in a glass bowl with all layers in full view. Feel free to experiment with layers of your own, such as a stripe of guacamole or a band of mild green chiles or black olives.

One 10-ounce package pork chorizo

One 15- to 16-ounce can refried Mexican black beans with jalapeño chiles

One 3-ounce package cream cheese

1 ripe Hass avocado, peeled, pitted, and chopped

1½ cups prepared fresh pico de gallo

About 2 cups grated pepper Jack cheese (8 ounces)

1 cup sour cream

2 tablespoons minced fresh cilantro

Multicolor tortilla chips for serving

1   Heat a medium-size skillet over medium heat. Crumble or chop the chorizo and cook it for 5 to 7 minutes, or until browned, then drain on paper towels.

2   Mix together the black beans and cream cheese and place on the bottom of an 8-cup glass serving bowl.

3   Mix together half of the avocado and all of the pico de gallo in a small bowl. Spoon over the black beans. Top with half of the cheese, followed by the chorizo and the remaining avocado. Sprinkle the remaining cheese over the avocado and spread the sour cream over the top. Sprinkle with the cilantro. Cover and refrigerate for at least 4 hours and up to 2 days. Serve with the chips.

Roasted Eggplant, White Bean, and Ricotta Salata Dip

SERVES 12

Want to taste Tuscany on a cracker? One bite of this and you'll be transported to your villa in Chianti, where eggplant and white beans are served on a daily basis. Try garnishing the dip with a few drops of high-quality, rich olive oil, serve with Belgian endive spears, bread slices, or crackers, and accompany with a romantic straw-covered bottle of hearty Chianti.

CHEESE CHOICES: You could also use a soft goat cheese or an aged Asiago.

1 large eggplant (about 1¼ pounds)

One 15-ounce can cannellini beans, rinsed and drained

2 cloves garlic

4 pieces sun-dried tomato

2 tablespoons cider vinegar

½ cup grated Parmesan cheese (about 1⅔ ounces)

4 ounces grated or crumbled ricotta salata cheese (about 1 cup)

2 tablespoons minced fresh flat-leaf parsley

Salt and freshly ground black pepper to taste

1 Preheat the oven to 375°F.

2 Make several long slashes on the eggplant skin and place on an oiled or sprayed baking sheet. Bake for 45 minutes, or until collapsed and tender. Let cool completely. Peel and coarsely shred the eggplant by hand.

3 Place the eggplant, beans, garlic, tomatoes, vinegar, and cheeses in a blender and pulse until smooth. Remove the mixture to a large bowl and stir in the parsley with a spatula. Season to taste with salt and pepper and serve.

The Maui Wowi

Anyone who's had the good fortune to spend time in the Hawaiian islands knows the sweet Maui onion that you can practically eat like an apple. Take heart, because during certain times of the year, they are easily found on the mainland. With Mauis, you can use the raw onion without sautéing it. The slightly crunchy texture of the onion with the creamy cheese is divine in this warm dip. If you can't find goat's milk Brie, regular is fine. Serve with pita chips, sturdy crackers, or roasted potato slices.

1 Maui onion, cut into ¼-inch dice

1 small red bell pepper, diced

½ of an 8-ounce package cream cheese, softened

One 10-ounce goat's milk Brie cheese, rind removed

2 tablespoons grated Parmesan cheese

2 tablespoons mayonnaise

2 tablespoons minced fresh basil

1   Preheat the oven to 425°F.

2   Lightly mix together the onion, pepper, cheeses, mayonnaise, and basil in a 2-quart soufflé or baking dish. Bake for about 10 minutes. Stir the dip, and then bake for an additional 5 minutes, or until golden brown. Serve piping hot.

Spicy Ale Fondue

SERVES 8

Planning a backyard Oktoberfest this season? Ask any serious beer drinker and you'll learn that cheese and ale together are the best thing since the arrival of hops. Experiment with different brews for the fondue. Chimay cheese from Belgium is an excellent choice for the pot if you can find it. Be sure to have your favorite pretzels nearby for dipping.

6 cups shredded mild Chimay, Monterey Jack, or German beer cheese (1½ pounds)

¼ cup all-purpose flour

One 12-ounce bottle dark ale

1 teaspoon dry mustard

1 small bunch fresh flat-leaf parsley, chopped

1 teaspoon red pepper flakes

Salt and freshly ground black pepper to taste

1   Preheat the broiler.

2   Place the cheese and flour in a large bowl and toss to combine.

3   Heat the ale in a fondue pot over medium-low heat just until it boils, and then add 1 cup of the cheese mixture, stirring constantly until the cheese has melted. Add the remaining cheese in 3 additions, stirring each time to melt the cheese. After all the cheese is incorporated, add the parsley and red pepper flakes. Taste the fondue and season with salt and pepper.

4   Broil the fondue until the top is golden and slightly flecked with brown. Set the fondue pot over tea lights and serve immediately.

Caesar Takes a Dip

SERVES 4

Looking for a stand-up way to serve the famous salad? Serve this Caesar dip with a platter of small, crisp romaine leaves and a bowl of dippable croutons—thinly sliced and toasted baguettes. Of course, the dip is also super with raw or grilled veggies, crackers, or chips.

1 large clove garlic, minced

1 teaspoon anchovy paste

1 tablespoon Dijon mustard

1 teaspoon Worcestershire sauce

2 tablespoons fresh lemon juice

2 tablespoons mayonnaise

½ cup extra-virgin olive oil

¼ cup grated Parmesan cheese (about ¾ ounce)

Freshly ground black pepper to taste

1   Place the garlic, anchovy paste, mustard, Worcestershire sauce, lemon juice, and mayonnaise in a blender. Blend until well mixed, then add the oil slowly. Blend until the dip has emulsified.

2   Remove to a bowl and stir in the cheese. Season generously with pepper. Serve immediately, or refrigerate in an airtight container for up to 1 week.

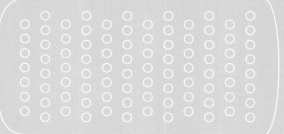

Warm and Tangy Shrimp Spread

SERVES 6

Creamy, luscious, and voluptuous—and all yours, with just a few ingredients. To gild the lily, substitute cooked crab or lobster for the shrimp. This is a chic appetizer to serve hot with thinly sliced country bread or, for an assemble-ahead treat, make it beforehand and serve it cold, spread on endive leaves or with crackers.

8 ounces cream cheese, at room temperature
¼ cup chopped onion
2 tablespoons sour cream
1 tablespoon prepared creamy horseradish
1 tablespoon minced fresh dill
8 ounces cooked shrimp, peeled and chopped
Salt and freshly ground black pepper to taste

1   Preheat the oven to 375°F. Oil a shallow 8-inch (1-quart) baking dish.

2   In a large bowl, beat together the cream cheese, onion, sour cream, and horseradish. Stir in the dill and shrimp and season with salt and pepper. Place in the prepared pan and bake for 20 minutes, or until bubbly.

3   Serve hot or cold.

Verrine of Goat Cheese and Fruit

SERVES 8

Verrines are all the rage in Paris these days. Read it as "terrine with a twist." In the windows of Fauchon, Paris's specialty food shop, you'll find small glasses with all kinds of treats inside. I loved a gorgeous one filled with layers of goat cheese and lots of berries. Serve with a flute of Prosecco or a sweet Moscato.

8 ounces fresh goat cheese

2 tablespoons honey

1 pint strawberries, hulled and sliced

1 pint blueberries, picked over for stems

8 sprigs fresh mint, for garnish

Tea biscuits or sweet crackers for serving

Place the cheese and honey in a medium-size bowl and beat with a hand mixer into a fluffy mixture. Spoon a layer of cheese into 8 small wine or cocktail glasses or large shot glasses, top with a berry layer, then finish with a cheese layer. Top each glass with a mint sprig. Serve with tea biscuits.

The Blue Moose

SERVES 6

Voilà: a mousse that will capture your cheese-loving heart. Currants are sweet, yet just tart enough to keep this a starter rather than a dessert. To match the richness of the mascarpone, try a creamy Cambozola or a pungent Gorgonzola for the blue cheese. Serve little clusters of Champagne grapes, sliced pears, endive leaves, and crackers alongside.

¼ cup dried currants

2 tablespoons port

8 ounces mascarpone cheese (1 cup)

½ cup crumbled or mashed blue cheese (about 2 ounces)

¼ cup sour cream

1   Place the currants and port in a microwavable dish and microwave for about 45 seconds on medium-high power, just until hot. Set aside to cool.

2   Place the cheeses and sour cream in a medium-size bowl and beat together thoroughly. Fold in the cooled currants and port, and spoon the mousse into a serving dish. Refrigerate for at least 3 hours.

3   Serve at room temperature.

Hungarian Liptauer Cheese

SERVES 6

My grandma Mazy, a Hungarian emigrant, used to tell me delicious food yarns of the old country. Liptauer cheese was often mentioned, usually followed by heated debate regarding the current state of paprika, etc. Now, decades later, I think she would be nodding approvingly of the pinjur addition to the mixture. Pinjur is a puree of eggplant, garlic, and peppers. Here's the new-millennium version of Mazy's Liptauer.

2 tablespoons drained capers

1 clove garlic

1 tablespoon sweet Hungarian paprika

2 teaspoons caraway seeds

8 ounces cream cheese, at room temperature

¼ cup sour cream

1 tablespoon pinjur, or ½ of a roasted red pepper, minced

2 tablespoons fresh lemon juice

1 teaspoon Dijon mustard

1 teaspoon anchovy paste

1   Place the capers and garlic in a mini food processor and pulse until minced. Or, mince the capers and garlic together with a knife.

2   In a small dry saucepan, toast the paprika and caraway seeds for 1 minute over medium-high heat, or until the seeds just begin to pop. Remove from the heat.

3   Place the caper mixture and toasted spices in a medium-size bowl and stir in the cheese, sour cream, pinjur, lemon juice, mustard, and anchovy paste and blend until smooth. Serve immediately, or cover and refrigerate for up to 1 week.

Italian Cheese Torta

SERVES 8

Here's a softer Mediterranean version of a savory torta. Usually these creations are held together with commercial cream cheese. It's more authentic and certainly more delectable with good-quality ricotta. If you have the opportunity, order ricotta and goat's cheese from Beaver Brook Farm (beaverbrookfarm.com). The farm, in Connecticut, sells a treasure trove of hand-made cow's and goat's milk cheeses. Serve this with crisp breadsticks or hunks of warm Italian bread.

One 8-ounce fresh goat cheese flavored with herbs

One 15-ounce container whole-milk ricotta cheese

⅓ cup grated Parmesan cheese (about 1 ounce)

½ cup prepared artichoke antipasto, chopped

½ cup slivered oil-packed sun-dried tomatoes

½ cup pine nuts, toasted

1   Mix the goat, ricotta, and Parmesan cheeses together in a large bowl.

2   Line a medium-size bowl with plastic wrap. Oil the plastic and place one-third of the cheese mixture in the bottom, pushing it up the sides. Top with the artichokes and half of the remaining cheese mixture. Top with the sun-dried tomatoes and the remaining cheese.

3   Cover with plastic wrap and refrigerate for at least 3 hours.

4   Unmold the torta to a serving platter, remove the plastic wrap, and press the pine nuts over the top and sides. Serve at room temperature.

The Classic Retro Cheese Ball

From the best of the archives comes this classic *fromage* ball that is still a crowd-pleaser. Serve it with sesame crackers and a crock of strong black olives that you've baked with red wine, garlic, and fennel seeds until just warmed through.

SERVES 4

1¾ cups shredded cheddar or smoked Gouda cheese (½ pound), at room temperature

3 ounces cream cheese, softened

1 tablespoon butter, softened

2 tablespoons mayonnaise

½ teaspoon Worcestershire sauce

½ of a medium-size shallot, minced (1 tablespoon)

¼ cup chopped pecans

2 teaspoons sweet paprika

½ cup finely chopped walnuts

1   Place the cheddar and cream cheeses, butter, and mayonnaise in a large bowl and beat together thoroughly. Stir in the Worcestershire, shallot, and pecans.

2   Form the sticky mixture into a ball. Place the paprika in a small strainer and dust it over the ball. Place the walnuts on a plate and roll the ball in the nuts. Wrap the cheese ball in plastic wrap or waxed paper and refrigerate for at least 1½ hours.

3   Unwrap the cheese ball, place on a plate, and serve at room temperature.

VARIATION #1:
Add ¼ cup Prosecco or sparkling wine to the cheeses and roll the ball in toasted pistachios or a combination of your favorite nuts and chopped golden raisins.

VARIATION #2:
For a spicy version, add a few drops of Tabasco or other hot sauce, half of a minced jalapeño, and ½ teaspoon ground cumin to the cheese mixture. Roll the cheese ball in minced fresh cilantro and ground pumpkin seeds.

Loxstock and Bagels

SERVES 6

Are lox and bagels a tradition on your Sunday morning breakfast table? Good enough! Try this very chic rendition of the tried and true. Remember to serve a large basket of toasted mini bagels alongside.

8 ounces cream cheese

1½ ounces mild goat cheese

2 teaspoons dried dillweed

1 tablespoon minced capers

3 ounces sliced smoked salmon

Juice of 1 medium-size lemon

1   Beat the cream and goat cheeses and the dillweed together in a medium-size bowl.

2   Line a 2-cup (2½ x 3 x 5½ inches) loaf pan with plastic wrap, letting the wrap overhang the sides generously. Oil the wrap. Spread 2 tablespoons of the cheese mixture in the pan. Top with 1 teaspoon of the capers and 1 ounce of the salmon. Sprinkle the salmon with a little lemon juice. Repeat this process twice, using the remaining cheese, capers, and salmon. Fold the top of the plastic wrap over the top of the pan and refrigerate for at least 6 hours.

3   To unmold, invert the pan onto a platter and remove the plastic wrap. Serve immediately.

INDEX

MEASUREMENT EQUIVALENTS

PLEASE NOTE THAT ALL CONVERSIONS ARE APPROXIMATE.

Liquid Conversions

U.S.	IMPERIAL	METRIC
1 tsp		5 ml
1 tbs	½ fl oz	15 ml
2 tbs	1 fl oz	30 ml
3 tbs	1½ fl oz	45 ml
¼ cup	2 fl oz	60 ml
⅓ cup	2½ fl oz	75 ml
⅓ cup + 1 tbs	3 fl oz	90 ml
⅓ cup + 2 tbs	3½ fl oz	100 ml
½ cup	4 fl oz	120 ml
⅔ cup	5 fl oz	150 ml
¾ cup	6 fl oz	180 ml
¾ cup + 2 tbs	7 fl oz	200 ml
1 cup	8 fl oz	240 ml
1 cup + 2 tbs	9 fl oz	275 ml
1¼ cups	10 fl oz	300 ml
1⅓ cups	11 fl oz	325 ml
1½ cups	12 fl oz	350 ml
1⅔ cups	13 fl oz	375 ml
1¾ cups	14 fl oz	400 ml
1¾ cups + 2 tbs	15 fl oz	450 ml
2 cups (1 pint)	16 fl oz	475 ml
2½ cups	20 fl oz	600 ml
3 cups	24 fl oz	720 ml
4 cups (1 quart)	32 fl oz	945 ml
		(1,000 ml is 1 liter)

Weight Conversions

U.S./U.K.	METRIC
½ oz	14 g
1 oz	28 g
1½ oz	43 g
2 oz	57 g
2½ oz	71 g
3 oz	85 g
3½ oz	100 g
4 oz	113 g
5 oz	142 g
6 oz	170 g
7 oz	200 g
8 oz	227 g
9 oz	255 g
10 oz	284 g
11 oz	312 g
12 oz	340 g
13 oz	368 g
14 oz	400 g
15 oz	425 g
1 lb	454 g

Oven Temperature Conversions

°F	GAS MARK	°C
250	½	120
275	1	140
300	2	150
325	3	165
350	4	180
375	5	190
400	6	200
425	7	220
450	8	230
475	9	240
500	10	260
550	Broil	290

ABOUT THE AUTHOR

Hallie Harron, a professional chef and restaurant consultant, is the co-author of *Tomatoes & Mozzarella* and a contributor to several other cookbooks, including the newly revised *The Joy of Cooking*. She has written for and been featured in numerous magazines, including *Bon Appétit*, *Food & Wine*, *Cooking Pleasures*, *Phoenix Magazine*, and *Phoenix Home & Garden*. Hallie has owned and operated several resturants, including the award-winning Quiessence in Phoenix, Arizona. She splits her time between Encinitas, California, and France, where she conducts food and wine tours to Paris and Provence.